DO ANIMALS GO TO SCHOOL?

This edition published 1997 by
Benchmark Books
Marshall Cavendish Corporation
99 White Plains Road
Tarrytown, New York 10591-9001

Devised and produced by Tucker Slingsby Ltd,
London House, 66-68 Upper Richmond Road,
London SW15 2RP

Designed by Helen James
Color separations by Positive Colour, Maldon, Essex, Great Britain
Printed and bound in Italy

ISBN 0–7614-0496-1

Library of Congress Cataloging-in-Publication Data

Parker, Steve.
    Do animals go to school? / by Steve Parker.
        p.   cm. -- (Ask about animals)
    Includes index.
    Summary: Explains animal behavior and the different ways in which
animals learn.
    ISBN 0-7614-0496-1 (lib. bdg.)
    1. Animal behavior--Juvenile literature. 2. Learning in animals -
-Juvenile literature.   [1. Animals--Habits and behavior.
2. Learning in animals.]   I. Title. II. Series: Parker, Steve.
Ask about animals.
QL751.5.P37 1997
591.51--dc20
                                                96-13345
                                                    CIP
                                                    AC

DO ANIMALS GO
TO SCHOOL?

Steve Parker

Illustrated by Graham Rosewarne

BENCHMARK BOOKS

MARSHALL CAVENDISH
NEW YORK

Introduction

Do you think animals go to school? Of course not! They don't sit at desks or learn to read, write, and count as you do. But think a bit harder. At school you learn things that will be important for the rest of your life. Although animals don't go to school in a special building, they do have to learn important lessons to survive.

Animals learn to catch and store food, make nests, fight against enemies, and find their way around. Sometimes their parents teach them. Sometimes they learn by themselves. They often make mistakes, just as we do.

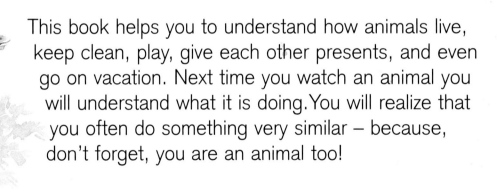

This book helps you to understand how animals live, keep clean, play, give each other presents, and even go on vacation. Next time you watch an animal you will understand what it is doing. You will realize that you often do something very similar – because, don't forget, you are an animal too!

Contents

DO ANIMALS...
Go to school?

Many animals are born tiny and helpless. They can do almost nothing except eat, sleep, and grow... just like you when you were a baby. As animals get older, they must learn all kinds of important skills, such as how to hunt and how to escape from danger. Some animals learn from their parents. Others, such as bugs, know what to do from the day they are born. This knowledge is called instinct, but animals still need to practice their skills to make sure they get it right.

These caterpillars are looking for a safe place to spend the night. They are called **processionary moth caterpillars** because they walk in a long line, called a procession. The leader makes sure no one gets lost by leaving a trail of smelly liquid along the branches. So the most important lesson for these caterpillars to learn is to follow their noses!

Chimpanzees learn quickly and they can also solve tricky problems. Young chimps learn to poke sticks into the nests of small insects called termites. They pull out the sticks and lick off the juicy termites. Chimpanzees learn how to do this from their parents and other group members. They may also discover how to use leaves and stones as tools.

Honey bees have many different jobs. First, they learn to clean out their hive. Then they practice flapping their wings and blowing air around the hive to keep it cool. Finally, they discover how to collect sweet, sticky nectar from flowers.

Collector bee

Cooler bee

Cleaner bee

Snow geese go to flying school. Every year, these beautiful birds fly to the far north, where they build nests and have their young. Then, before the cold winter, they fly back to the south. For the first few years, young birds follow the older ones who have made the journey before. The youngsters learn to recognize the rivers, mountains, coastlines, islands, and other places on their trip. Soon they are able to find the way on their own.

Baby **otters** have fun splashing around in rivers, playing with sticks and stones. But they are actually learning to be champion swimmers. They need to dart through the water to catch fresh fish. If they don't work hard, they will end up with nothing for dinner.

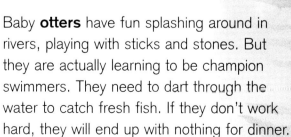

DO ANIMALS...
Go on vacation?

Most people like to travel to sunny places for their vacations. Animals do too. Many creatures leave cold countries to go somewhere warm for several months each year. Their long journeys are called migrations. Once they arrive, they can rest and feed. Some animals never stay in one place for long. They are always on the move and every day is a new holiday adventure.

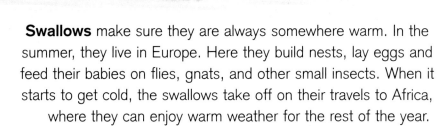

Swallows make sure they are always somewhere warm. In the summer, they live in Europe. Here they build nests, lay eggs and feed their babies on flies, gnats, and other small insects. When it starts to get cold, the swallows take off on their travels to Africa, where they can enjoy warm weather for the rest of the year.

These animals are called **reindeer**. During spring and summer they live in the cold, open lands of northern Europe. When autumn comes, it is too cold even for them, so they go on a winter vacation. They head south in large herds. As the snow melts in spring they walk north again, eating the new, juicy plants as they go.

Beautiful **monarch butterflies** are sun-seekers. As summer ends in Canada and the USA they fly south. Some go as far as Mexico. Here thousands of them rest through the warm winter, clustering on cliffs, trees, and cave walls. Next summer they will fly north again.

Polar bears can't leave home to go on vacation because they have no homes. They are on the move all the time, journeying across the snow or swimming in the icy seas, looking for seals to eat. During the coldest weather, female polar bears do dig a hole in the snow and they give birth to their cubs in this den.

Some animals' vacations are mystery tours – at least they are a mystery to us! Every autumn in the Caribbean, **spiny lobsters** march in long processions across the sea bed. Slowly, they make their way towards deeper water. Nobody really knows why. Perhaps they are going away to escape stormy seas and strong currents. In a few months they will be back in the shallower seas.

Live in towns and cities?

Adults and children all over the world live in towns and cities. In some cities there are millions of people. Many other creatures live together in big groups, too. Usually animals that live together are good neighbors and all work for the benefit of the whole town. They collect and store food, build and look after homes, find new partners, raise their families, and chase away enemies. But, just as in the towns and cities where people live, there are sometimes arguments and even fights.

Welcome to wasp city. It is a nest the size of a basketball with about 1,000 **wasps** inside. Wasps build the nest from paper that they make from wood. First they scrape up the wood with their jaws. Then they chew it into a sticky liquid. Finally the wasps spread out this liquid, which hardens to make the papery nest walls. Wasps build their nest cities inside a roof or hollow tree.

Puffins are tubby sea birds with big heads and colorful beaks. They nest together in "towns", called colonies, along the seashore. Here, most puffin parents dig a burrow for their eggs. Others take over a spare rabbit hole or a tunnel left by another sea bird. Puffin colonies are always noisy places, full of activity.

10

On the grasslands of North America, small heads sometimes pop out of holes in mounds of earth. These heads belong to **prairie dogs**. They make dog-like barks, but they are really a type of squirrel. Each prairie dog family has its own entrance hole leading to its own set of long, deep burrows. More than 10,000 prairie dogs may live in one township. Prairie dog sentries guard the burrows. If they see an enemy, they lift up their heads and bark a warning to all the other inhabitants of the town.

Termites are tiny, soft insects. They live together in groups of over a million. Their cities, called termite mounds, have more inhabitants than any others in the animal world. Inside these giant heaps of hard mud and earth, there are many tunnels and chambers. Here the termites are safe from enemies. The mounds can be twice as high as a person. They're termite skyscrapers!

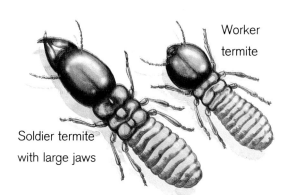

Worker
termite

Soldier termite
with large jaws

11

DO ANIMALS...
Have houses?

Many animals do live in houses, but they are not built of brick or lumber with glass windows like the house you probably live in. Animal houses are usually made of wood, mud or stones. They shelter animals from bad weather and from enemies. Animals can rest, eat, and store food there. They often raise a family inside, too. Some animals build a new home each year. Others keep the same home for most of their lives.

Look into a pond in summer. You may see what look like stones crawling along the bottom. This is the tube-shaped house of a **caddisfly larva**, the young of the caddisfly. These larvae make their homes from leaves, sticks, or pebbles, which they glue together with a slimy liquid. The head and legs of the caddisfly larva poke out at one end.

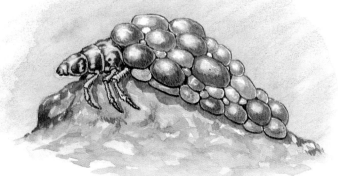

Eagles have very spacious homes. They build the biggest nests of any bird, perching them high on a cliff ledge or in a tall tree. The nests, called eyries, are huge piles of sticks and twigs. A mother and father eagle may have several eyries. Each year they choose one to live in, then add more twigs to make it bigger and stronger. Some eyries are as large as a small car!

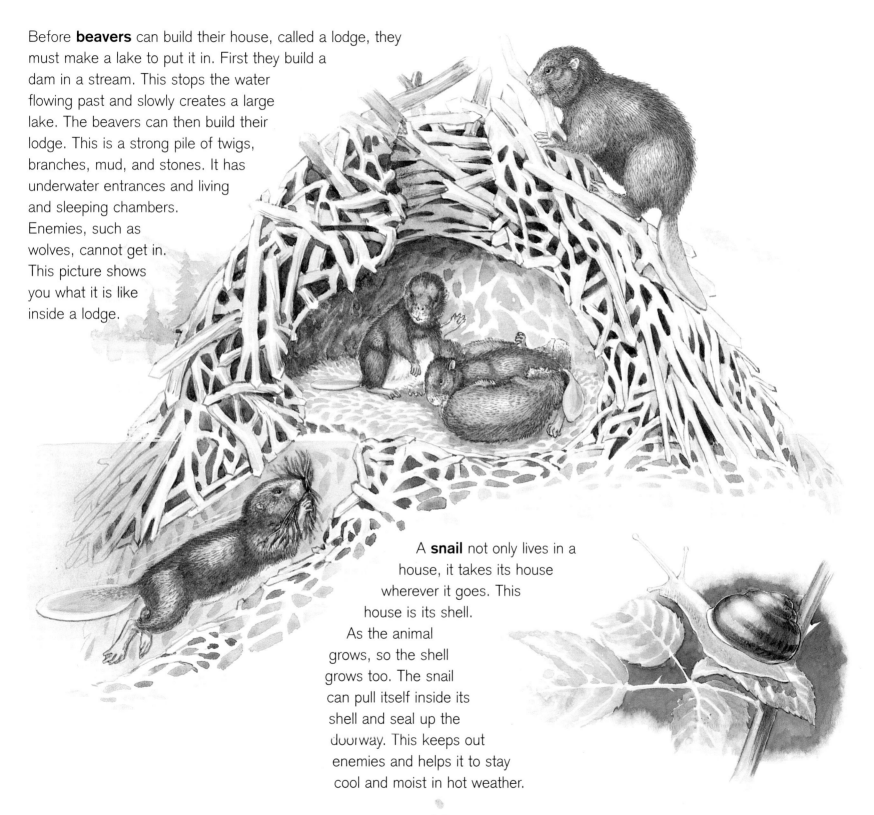

Before **beavers** can build their house, called a lodge, they must make a lake to put it in. First they build a dam in a stream. This stops the water flowing past and slowly creates a large lake. The beavers can then build their lodge. This is a strong pile of twigs, branches, mud, and stones. It has underwater entrances and living and sleeping chambers. Enemies, such as wolves, cannot get in. This picture shows you what it is like inside a lodge.

A **snail** not only lives in a house, it takes its house wherever it goes. This house is its shell. As the animal grows, so the shell grows too. The snail can pull itself inside its shell and seal up the doorway. This keeps out enemies and helps it to stay cool and moist in hot weather.

13

Have baths and showers?

You probably wash your face each morning and evening. Perhaps you have a bath or shower with soap or gel. This helps to get rid of dirt, dust, and body smells and cleans your hair, skin, and nails. Animals keep themselves clean, too. They may use water or mud, or their tongues, fingers, or claws. They may even get a friend to help.

The **housefly** paddles in dirt and muck and when it eats it licks up all kinds of disgusting things. But if you watch a fly you will probably see it rubbing its legs together and brushing its head or wings. Despite its filthy habits, it is a clean insect.

Elephants love to squirt water over themselves. This helps to keep them cool in the hot sun. They also like to bathe – in mud! The mud helps to get rid of flies and pests that irritate the elephant's skin. The mud also dries to form an extra "skin". This protects the elephant against sunburn and biting insects.

All cats keep themselves clean. They have very rough tongues, like sandpaper, to lick dirt and pests from their fur. This **leopard** is washing its face. It rubs one paw over its face to remove mud, leaves, and insects, then licks the paw to make it clean.

Like most birds, the **jay** combs and cleans its feathers with its beak. Sometimes lice and other pests get under the feathers and grab on to the bird's skin. So the jay gets some help. It squats in an ants' nest or holds ants in its beak. The ants nip the lice and pests from the jay's skin.

Most baby animals cannot wash themselves, so their mother usually does it for them. The mother **fox**, called a vixen, licks her cubs clean. The fox family lives in a large hole, called a den, until the cubs are several weeks old. The mother keeps the den clean, too. She carries droppings and old bedding outside in her mouth.

15

DO ANIMALS...
Have refrigerators?

People keep their food fresh in gleaming refrigerators. Animals don't have these, of course, but many creatures do store food in special hiding places, to make sure they have enough to eat all year round. In autumn, when trees are covered with fruits, nuts, and berries, animals collect and bury food for the long winter ahead. If you had to collect or hunt for food, instead of buying it from the store, you might do the same!

A **squirrel** rushes about in the autumn gathering nuts and burying them here, there, and everywhere. During the winter, when the trees are bare, the squirrel sniffs and digs, and finds perhaps half of the nuts it hid. The other nuts are not all wasted. Some grow into new trees.

A **crocodile** sometimes catches a zebra or an antelope. This is far too big for one meal. So the crocodile eats as much as it can, then pushes the leftovers under a rock or log in the river. The meat stays safely in place and softens in the warm water. A few days later, the croc comes back for a second helping.

16

To stop food from going bad, people store it in a refrigerator or freezer. The **Arctic fox** scrapes a hole and buries its food in the frozen ground. But the fox does not have a microwave oven or stove to thaw its meal of Arctic hare, lemming, or small bird. It simply digs up the food, then waits until the frozen meal melts in its mouth.

If some animals didn't eat droppings and dung, the world would be full of it! The favorite food of the **dung beetle** is warm, moist, freshly produced dung. The beetle rolls dung up in a ball, lays eggs in it, and hides the ball in a burrow. When the eggs hatch, the beetle grubs have their food waiting.

The **shrike** is a fierce hunter of insects, small lizards, frogs, mice, and other little creatures. On a good day, it catches more victims than it can eat at once. So it sticks the extra ones on to thorns or plant spines, then comes back later for a snack. This gruesome larder of hanging meat gives the shrike its other name – the butcher bird.

17

DO ANIMALS...
Eat take-out meals?

If people do not want to cook a meal, they can order food from a take-out restaurant. When it is ready, they carry the food home in special containers. Some animals also collect their food packed in containers, ready to eat, and perhaps still warm. But the containers are hairy or scaly and there are often bits of bone in the food. Animals cannot just order food – they have to catch their take-out meals before they can carry them home.

A mouse, vole, or lemming is a small snack for a grown-up **owl**, but the same victim makes a meal for an owl chick. The parent owls are busy all night. They swoop through the dark to grab furry bundles of food, which they carry back to a nestful of hungry owlets.

In North America, **raccoons** sometimes visit houses and search through garbage cans. These animals sniff around everywhere, looking for leftover food. Raccoons will eat almost anything, from bites of burger to chicken bones and French fries. Often they grab scraps from take-out meal cartons and hurry away with them – secondhand take-outs!

Rabbits don't take their food home, but they certainly eat it from special containers! Rabbits spend many hours nibbling grass and leaves, and take in goodness from them. They get rid of the leftovers as small, round droppings on the ground. Later, they eat these droppings to take in any minerals they missed the first time round. When the rabbits produce droppings for the second time, these are much drier and harder.

The **bolas spider** does not spin a web. Instead it hangs around on a twig or rock, waiting for unwary insects to wander past. Then it leaps out, lassoes an insect with a silk rope, and ties its prey into a neat bundle. The spider's name comes from the bolas, a rope with weights at the end that South American cowboys use to trip up cattle.

The favorite take-out of the **fisherman bat** is fish. Almost every evening the bat swoops over rivers and lakes, watching for ripples made by fish just below the surface. Then it grabs a victim with its long-clawed feet and flies away to a tree. There it tears the meat from its instant, slippery, scaly snack.

Have babysitters?

Like human parents, animal parents sometimes get very busy. They may have to leave their young for a while, to hunt for food or chase away enemies. When human parents go out, friends or relatives, such as aunts and uncles, may look after the children. Some animals do the same, but babysitting is not very common in the animal world. It mainly happens among creatures that live in large groups.

This tiny **robin** is feeding a big baby cuckoo. Of course, she is not its real mother. The mother cuckoo always lays her egg in the nest of another bird, then flies away. When the baby cuckoo hatches, it pushes the other bird's eggs from the nest. The robin thinks the cuckoo chick is hers. So she and her mate keep feeding it until the "baby" is many times bigger than they are!

Meerkats live in long, winding burrows in the grasslands of Africa. They eat all kinds of food, from insects, lizards, birds, and other small creatures to leaves, seeds, and fruits. In a large group of about 30 meerkats there will be several families. The adults take turns looking after one another's young, so parents can go and look for food or defend the burrows against enemies.

When baby birds hatch, the first thing they usually see is their real mother. They follow her everywhere. But sometimes eggs get mixed up. A hen may sit on a duck's eggs by mistake. When the **ducklings** hatch, they see the hen and think she is their mother. Soon they start to walk behind her in a line. The hen has become their new mother, even though she may not want to be!

Giraffes are the tallest animals in the world. With their long legs and long necks, they can reach leaves high up in the trees. When parent giraffes go off to find food, they may leave their young behind. These babies gather in a group, called a crèche. Sometimes "aunties" babysit for the young giraffes to make sure they don't get into trouble.

21

DO ANIMALS...
Stay home alone?

Yes, they do. In fact, in the animal world, it is natural and very common for young animals to be left alone. They stay in the nest or burrow while the parents go out to feed. The babies are usually well hidden and know by instinct that they must stay quiet to remain safe from their enemies. Could you stay quiet for half a day until your parents came back? You probably could if your life depended on it!

A young **deer** is called a fawn. Unlike its parents, the fawn has white spots on its fur. As it lies in the grass under a bush, the fawn's pattern merges with the shadows and patches of sunlight. This makes it very hard for enemies to spot the fawn. The mother deer is away feeding, but she will soon return.

The **albatross** is a huge, white sea bird with very long wings. The baby albatross is a large ball of fluffy feathers. Its parents fly over the sea for two or three weeks catching fish. They leave the chick alone on a cold, windy island. But there is a reward. The parents bring back smelly, half-digested fish for their baby to eat.

Baby **penguins** are born in the coldest place on Earth, the ice-covered land of Antarctica. Even a freezer is warmer! The parent penguins waddle off and dive into the ocean to catch fish and other sea animals. The babies are left home alone and stay in a group, huddled together against the cold. They don't need to worry about enemies. It is too cold for any other animals.

Usually, a young **kangaroo** lives in its mother's pouch, which is a pocket of skin on her front. The baby only comes out to play or feed. But the mother may sometimes have to bound away very quickly to avoid enemies. Then she leaves her baby hiding in a bush, so that she can run faster. She returns later to collect her baby.

The **platypus** has webbed feet, a furry body, and a mouth like a duck's bill. It lives in rivers and lakes in eastern Australia. Baby platypuses live in a long tunnel, which the mother digs in a river bank. When she goes out to eat, the mother blocks the burrow entrance with mud. The babies are alone, but safely locked in.

23

DO ANIMALS...
Dance and sing?

It is great fun to go to a party and dance and sing. Animals love to party too, but not just for fun. In the spring, adult animals begin their courtship. This means they try to attract a mate, often by putting on song-and-dance displays. The males are usually the ones to sing and dance. Sometimes their skin, fur, or feathers change color, too. Their calls and movements may seem strange to us. But to the females these performances are too good to miss!

Ree-deep, ree-deep. Rivet-rivet. Wurp-wurp. It's spring again and the chorus of male **frogs** fills the evening air. The males gather in ponds and swamps to croak and croon love songs to the females. Each type of frog has a different call. Soon the females arrive to choose the best male of their type as a mate.

One of nature's most spectacular sights is the courtship display of male **birds of paradise**. These birds live in the tropical forests of Southeast Asia. They sing loudly, shake their brilliant feathers, hop about, and sometimes even hang upside down from branches. The dull brown females watch the splendid performance.

24

Koalas live in the gum trees of eastern Australia. The male koala doesn't really sing, but he does make a deep, bellowing, growling noise. This noise echoes through the night air. He is telling other male koalas to keep away from his patch of forest, otherwise he'll fight them. He is also asking female koalas if they would like to come over to his tree!

After their long winter sleep, **snakes** shake themselves and slither around in the warmth of spring. Several males gather around one female, who is bigger than they are. The males sway and hiss and try to twine around her in a loving dance. The female chooses the healthiest, and most persistent, male as her mate.

Moans, grunts, and squeals drift through the waters of the world's oceans. They are the cries of whales singing for mates. Male **humpback whales** sing to tell female humpbacks that they are nearby and available to be fathers. The males also slap their flippers and tails on to the surface of the water. This must be the world's slowest, heaviest courtship dance.

25

DO ANIMALS...
Go to the doctor?

Animals sometimes get ill and hurt themselves, just as you do. But they can't go to a doctor or dentist, because there isn't one. Instead, animals have to look after themselves. They know by instinct what to do. They may eat or drink something that works like a kind of medicine or they may lick and clean a wound. Animals know that they should lie quietly and rest to help them get better. You probably know how hard it is to do this for more than a few minutes!

The main food of **butterflies** is the sweet, honey-like nectar in flowers. But these beautiful insects also need other substances, such as minerals and vitamins, to stay healthy. So from time to time, they sip at a pool of animal urine, which contains many minerals. Luckily for us, we can buy vitamin and mineral tablets from a store.

Even a small cut can be very dangerous for a **hippopotamus**. Hippos live in muddy rivers, so if a cut is not covered up and the water is dirty, the injury can become infected and never heal. To avoid this the hippo rolls in wet earth to cover and protect the wound. Its bandage is made of mud!

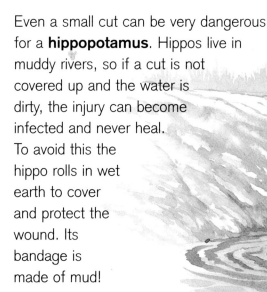

Macaws and other parrots are colorful, tropical birds. They eat leaves, fruits, nuts, and seeds. Some also feed on small animals, such as insects and worms. If they don't eat enough different foods, they become ill. Then macaws prescribe their own medicine. They fly to special, soft rocks that are full of minerals. There they scrape the rocks with their beaks and eat the mineral-rich rock dust.

Big fish sometimes get bits of food left in their mouths and blood-sucking pests become attached to their skin and scales. They can't go to a dentist or doctor. Small fish, called **cleaner wrasse**, nibble away the old food and pests for them. The wrasses even clean inside the fishes' mouths. The bigger fish could easily eat the cleaner wrasses, but they never do.

Dogs like to munch meat and crack bones, but if they start to feel sick they may eat grass. Then they are sick and this clears any bad or rotten food from their stomachs. The dog's wild cousin, the wolf, does exactly the same thing. When they feel ill, dogs and wolves know what to do by instinct. These are the feelings they are born with.

Give each other presents?

Some animals do give one another presents, but not on birthdays or during special festivals as people do. Creatures usually give presents to their mates when they are courting in spring. An adult sometimes gives its partner a surprise present at other times of the year, just to make sure he or she doesn't forget they are mates. Animal parents give "toys" to their babies to play with. Imagine how disappointed you would be if you opened a package to find just a twig or a stone.

The **right whale** baby is enormous, almost as big as a car. Its mother looks after it well and protects it from hungry enemies, such as sharks and killer whales. The mother may give her baby a present of a tree trunk that has floated out to sea. The baby whale has great fun playing with this huge "toy". It will bash it about in the water with its flippers and tail.

Some birds offer presents to their partners. The gifts are usually pieces of food, and they help the male and female to stay friends. The male **kingfisher** gives his mate a fish. He offers it head-first, so that she can swallow it without choking. These tasty presents help to keep the partners together.

The male **wolf spider** catches a fly or other insect and ties it with his silk thread. Then he gives this neatly wrapped parcel to the female. While she undoes the present and eats it, he quickly mates with her. The male spider is smaller than the female and, at mating time, she may eat him. So it is very important for the male not to forget this present!

Gibbons are long-armed apes that swing through the trees of Southeast Asia. Like many apes and monkeys they groom each other. This means that they comb and scratch through each other's fur and pick out dirt, leaves, and pests. They may offer the pests, such as lice and fleas, to each other to eat as tasty tidbits!

29

DO ANIMALS...
Clean up their homes?

Your parents probably do most of the cleaning at home. Animals know that they must clean out their nests and burrows, too. If they didn't, they would be deep in skin, feathers, or fur – not to mention fleas and piles of droppings! Many animals spend lots of time tidying their homes and removing rubbish. They have no vacuum cleaners or brushes. Instead, they use their feet, claws, and mouths.

Harvest mice live in a nest the size and shape of a tennis ball. It is made out of woven grass stems. The mother harvest mouse is always going in and out through the small entrance hole, carrying rubbish in her mouth. She is clearing out droppings and bits of leftover food that her babies have not eaten.

Badgers are well known as very clean animals. Every few days, they clear out their set. This is the name we give to their underground home of tunnels and rooms. The badgers pull out all the old leaves, grass, and moss, which they use for bedding. Then they collect clean, dry bedding and take it into the set.

30

Many birds use their beaks to flick bits of old food and droppings from their nests.
A **blue tit** nest may be occupied by more than ten chicks, who sometimes leave bits of their caterpillar dinners. The blue tit parents give the nest a good cleaning several times each day.

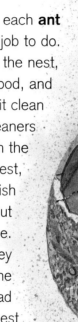

In an ants' nest, each **ant** has a special job to do. Soldiers protect the nest, foragers collect food, and cleaners keep it clean and neat. The cleaners scurry through the corridors in the nest, gathering rubbish and throwing it out of the entrance. Sometimes they have to collect the bodies of dead and dying nest members, too.

All **cats**, big and small, are neat and clean. They would never lie down to sleep on lumpy stones or sharp twigs. They remove any pieces of rubbish from their favorite resting place before settling down for a catnap. After all, would you sleep in a bed full of stones or sticks?

31

Pollute the world?

No. Only human animals do. We cut down forests, tunnel through mountains and cover the land with roads, houses, and buildings. We build factories, vehicles, and power stations that pollute the air, poison the soil and water, and destroy the natural places where plants and animals once lived. What do you imagine wild animals think about all this? Do you think that they want to be like us?

Index